For my sister Teresa

Extracts from the Authorized King James Version of the Bible,
the rights of which are vested in the Crown in perpetuity
within the United Kingdom, are reproduced by permission of
Eyre & Spottiswoode Publishers, Her Majesty's Printers, London.

The words are taken from

Matthew
26 : 14-17, 19, 20, 25-6, 34, 40, 42-3, 47-9, 52, 56, 62-3, 65-6, 73; 27 : 1-5,
11, 24, 26, 29, 31, 44, 51, 54, 57-60; 28 : 1, 19-20

Mark
11 : 8-10; 14 : 11, 18-19, 26, 36, 41-42, 44, 53-4, 62, 67; 15 : 2, 12-14,
25, 27, 43; 16 : 5

Luke
3 : 1; 22 : 7, 19-20, 34, 41-2, 44, 46, 48, 51, 54-60; 23 : 26-7, 33-4,
39-46, 55-6; 24 : 2

John
11 : 55; 12 : 1-5, 7, 12; 13 : 4-5, 12-14, 30, 34, 36-7; 18 : 10, 26, 38-40;
19 : 2-3, 25-7, 39; 20 : 2, 4, 8, 10-16, 18-20, 24-29

William Heinemann Limited
Michelin House, 81 Fulham Road, London SW3
LONDON   MELBOURNE   AUCKLAND

First Published 1989
Concept, design and illustration © Jan Pieńkowski 1989
0-434-95659-7

Easter

The King James Version
with pictures
by

Jan Pieńkowski

HEINEMANN : LONDON

IN THE REIGN of Tiberius Caesar, Pontius Pilate being governor of Judaea, many went up to Jerusalem for the Passover. And Jesus took the twelve disciples and came to Bethany where Lazarus was whom he raised from the dead. There they made him a supper, and Martha served.

Then took Mary a pound of ointment of spikenard, very costly, and anointed the feet of Jesus, and wiped his feet with her hair.

Then saith one of his disciples, Judas Iscariot, Why was not this ointment sold for three hundred pence, and given to the poor? Then said Jesus, Let her alone: against the day of my burying hath she done this.

Then Judas went to the chief priests, and said, What will ye give me and I will deliver him to you? And they promised to give him thirty pieces of silver.

And from that time he sought opportunity to betray him.

 N THE NEXT DAY much people that were
come to the feast, when they heard that Jesus
was coming to Jerusalem, spread their garments
in the way: and others cut down branches off the trees,
and strawed them in the way.

And they that went before, and they that followed, cried,
saying Hosanna! Blessed is he that cometh in the name of
the Lord! Hosanna in the highest!

possible unto thee; take away this cup from me; nevertheless not my will, but thine, be done.

And he cometh to the disciples and findeth them asleep, and saith unto Peter, What, could ye not watch with me one hour?

He went away again the second time and prayed. And being in an agony he prayed more earnestly: and his sweat was as it were great drops of blood falling down to the ground. And he came and found them asleep again: for their eyes were heavy.

And he cometh the third time, and saith to them, Why sleep ye? Rise up, let us go; lo, he that betrayeth me is at hand.

And while he yet spake, Judas came, and with him a great multitude with swords and staves, from the chief priests and leaders of the people.

He had given them a sign, saying, Whomsoever I shall kiss, that same is he: hold him fast. And forthwith he came to Jesus and said, Hail, master; and kissed him.

But Jesus said to him, Judas, betrayest thou the Son of man with a kiss?

THEN PETER having a sword drew it, and smote the high priest's servant, and cut off his right ear. Then said Jesus, Put up thy sword; for all they that take the sword shall perish with the sword. And he touched his ear, and healed him.

Then all the disciples forsook him, and fled.

They led Jesus away into the high priest's house. And Peter followed afar off and sat with the servants, and warmed himself at the fire.

But a certain maid earnestly looked upon him and said, Thou also wast with Jesus. And he denied, saying, Woman, I know him not.

After a little while another saw him, and said, Surely, thou also art one of them. And Peter said, Man, I am not.

And about one hour after one of the servants, being his kinsman whose ear Peter cut off, saith, Did not I see thee with him? And Peter said, Man, I know not what thou sayest.

And immediately the cock crew. And the Lord turned, and looked upon Peter.

And Peter went out, and wept bitterly.

AND THE HIGH PRIEST arose, and said Tell us whether thou be the Christ, the Son of God. And Jesus said, I am. Then the high priest rent his clothes, saying, Behold, now ye have heard his blasphemy, what think ye? They answered, He is guilty of death.

When morning was come, they led him away to Pontius Pilate.

Then Judas repented, and brought again the thirty pieces of silver to the chief priests and elders, saying, I have betrayed the innocent blood. And they said, What is that to us? see thou to that. And he cast down the pieces of silver and departed, and went and hanged himself.

JESUS STOOD before the governor: and the governor asked him, Art thou the King of the Jews? And Jesus said, Thou sayest it.

Pilate went out unto the Jews, and saith to them, I find in him no fault at all. But ye have a custom, that I should release unto you one at the passover: Will ye therefore that I release unto you the King of the Jews?

Then cried they all, Not this man but Barabbas.

Now Barabbas was a robber.

And Pilate said again to them, What will ye then that I shall do unto him whom ye call the King of the Jews? And they cried out, Crucify him. Then Pilate said, Why, what evil hath he done? And they cried out the more exceedingly, Crucify him.

When Pilate saw that he could prevail nothing, he took water, and washed his hands before the multitude, saying, I am innocent of the blood of this just person. Then released he Barabbas unto them: and when he had scourged Jesus, he delivered him to be crucified.

THE SOLDIERS platted a crown of thorns, and put it on his head, and they put on him a purple robe. And they bowed the knee before him saying, Hail, King of the Jews! And they smote him with their hands.

After they had mocked him they took the robe off from him and led him away to crucify him.

S THEY LED him away, they laid hold upon one Simon, a Cyrenian, coming out of the country, and on him they laid the cross, that he might bear it after Jesus.

And there followed him a great company of people and of women, which bewailed and lamented him.

And when they were come to the place which is called Calvary, there they crucified him, and with him two thieves; the one on his right hand, and the other on his left.

Then said Jesus, Father, forgive them: for they know not what they do.

And it was the third hour.

One of the thieves which were crucified with him railed on him, saying, If thou be Christ, save thyself and us. But the other rebuked him, saying, Dost not thou fear God? For we receive the due reward of our deeds: but this man hath done nothing amiss. And he said to Jesus, Lord, remember me when thou comest into thy kingdom.

And Jesus said to him, Today shalt thou be with me in paradise.

NOW THERE STOOD by the cross of Jesus his mother, and his mother's sister, and Mary Magdalene. When Jesus saw his mother and the disciple whom he loved, he saith to his mother, Woman, behold thy son! Then saith he to the disciple, Behold thy mother!

And from that hour that disciple took her unto his own home.

IT WAS about the sixth hour, and there was a darkness over all the earth until the ninth hour. The sun was darkened, and the veil of the temple was rent in twain from the top to the bottom; and the earth did quake, and the rocks rent.

And when Jesus had cried with a loud voice, he said, Father, into thy hands I commend my spirit: and having said thus, he gave up the ghost.

Now when the centurion, and they that were with him, saw the earthquake, they feared greatly, saying, Truly this was the Son of God.

When the even was come, there came a rich man of Arimathaea, named Joseph, who also was Jesus' disciple.

He went boldly to Pilate, and begged the body of Jesus. Then Pilate commanded the body to be delivered.

AND WHEN JOSEPH had taken the body, he wrapped it in a clean linen cloth with spices, myrrh and aloes, and laid it in his own new tomb which he had hewn out in the rock.

And he rolled a great stone to the door of the sepulchre, and departed.

AS IT BEGAN to dawn came Mary Magdalene
and found the stone rolled away. Then she
runneth to Peter, and to the other disciple,
and saith, They have taken away the Lord. So they ran to the
sepulchre, and saw, and believed.

Then the disciples went away to their home, but Mary
stood at the sepulchre weeping, and as she wept she saw two
angels sitting where the body of Jesus had lain. And they say,

Woman, why weepest thou? She saith, Because they have
taken away my Lord, and I know not where they have laid
him. And she turned and saw Jesus standing, and knew not
that it was Jesus.

Jesus saith, Woman, why weepest thou? whom seekest thou?
She, supposing him to be the gardener saith, Sir, if thou
have borne him hence, tell me where thou hast laid him.

Jesus saith unto her, Mary. She turned and saith unto him,
Rabboni; which is to say Master.

Mary Magdalene came and told the disciples.

THE SAME EVENING, when the disciples were assembled came Jesus and stood in the midst, and saith, Peace be unto you. Then were the disciples glad, when they saw the Lord.

But Thomas, one of the twelve, was not with them when Jesus came. The other disciples therefore said to him, We have seen the Lord. But he said to them, Except I see in his hands the print of the nails, and put my finger into the print of the nails, I will not believe.

And after eight days again his disciples were within, and Thomas with them. Then came Jesus, the doors being shut, and stood in the midst, and said to Thomas, Reach hither thy finger, and behold my hands; and be not faithless, but believing. And Thomas answered and said unto him, My Lord and my God.

Jesus saith to Thomas, Because thou hast seen me, thou hast believed; blessed are they that have not seen, and yet have believed.

GO YE THEREFORE, and teach all nations, baptizing them in the name of the Father, and of the Son, and of the Holy Ghost. And lo, I am with you alway, even unto the end of the world.